AF375218

Joni Mitchell Called Me Ugly

Persuasion and the Power of an Ask

By Timothy J. Boynton

Table of Contents

Dedication

This book is for my mother, Susan, whose absence has been the quiet echo behind every page, and whose love has been the compass guiding every ask, every risk, every leap of faith.

Each night, you sang "The Circle Game" to me as a lullaby, your voice weaving together tenderness and truth. Before I ever understood the lyrics, I understood their meaning: that life turns like seasons, that joy and sorrow chase one another, and that real, eternal love outlives us all.

That song became our bond – a sacred promise whispered in the dark – and it has carried me ever since.

You taught me that generosity is not measured in what we have, but in what we give: our laughter, our presence, our belief in others. You showed me how to lead with heart, how to see people fully, and how to love with a courage that even time could not undo.

Though you are gone, you live on in every page of this book, in every story of persuasion, and in every chance I dare to take. This book is my way of singing "The Circle Game" back to you, because your song never ended. It only changed voices.

Joni Mitchell Called Me Ugly

Foreword

By Julianna Margulies

I am living, breathing proof that Tim's methods of persuasion work.
After meeting Tim for the first time, he sent me a manuscript of this
book and asked if I would consider reading it. There was just something
so unexpected, so bold, so genuine about his ask that I just couldn't say
no.

Then came something he is so good at: The Ask.

When Tim asked me to write the foreword for this book, I smiled
immediately. Not because I had the perfect words at hand, but because
that's the effect Tim has on people: he asks, and you instinctively want
to say *yes*.

Over the course of my life, I've learned that true persuasion is not about
pressure, charm, or even charisma. It's about sincerity. It's about
showing people that they matter, that their story belongs to something
greater, and that their *yes* can change the world.

That's what Tim does. He persuades not with force, but with heart.

I know Tim builds bridges between people and causes that, at first, seem
impossible to connect. He turns difficult conversations into moments of
laughter, hesitation into confidence, and doubt into belief. He has the
rare gift of making people feel not only valued, but necessary; like their
role in the story is the one that matters most.

This book, *Joni Mitchell Called Me Ugly*, is Tim's love letter to that gift.

It's a reminder that persuasion is not manipulation; it's trust, courage, and vulnerability woven together. It's a reminder that the most powerful ask is really an invitation: "Come with me. You belong in this story."

As you turn these pages, you'll laugh, you may cry, but most importantly, you'll be reminded that the courage to ask and the grace to listen can change your work, your life, and maybe even your legacy.

Tim lives this truth every day, and now he's offering it to you. I'm so glad he asked me to introduce you to it.

Acknowledgments

This book is the result of more than words on a page; it's the sum of every person who has walked with me, believed in me, challenged me, and reminded me of what matters most. To each of you, I am deeply grateful.

For my father, who taught me that when good thoughts arrive, you must put pen to paper before they pass – as a true author, you showed me that words can carry legacies, if only we are brave enough to write them down.

For Alvin – you are my anchor and my joy, my greatest confidant and my truest companion. Your love has been the steady note beneath every melody of my life. With you, I have found not just a partner, but a reason. Everything I am most proud of in this world exists because of you.

For Piglet, our little heartbeat with fur – you remind me to laugh, play, rest, and greet each day with wonder.

For Mark, who first invited me into the world of storytelling on Broadway – our artistry opened a door I never could have imagined, and your mentorship gave me the courage to step through it.

For Danielle, my colleague, mentor, and friend – your faith in me has been both anchor and wind. You have shown me that leadership at its best is persuasion in service of others, grounded in vision, and elevated by generosity.

For Jodi, my right arm at work – your loyalty, brilliance, and heart have made my career not only meaningful, but deeply fulfilling.

For Bitty, my best friend and family in every sense of the word – with you, laughter becomes medicine, loyalty becomes unshakable, and life becomes brighter. You have a way of turning even the most ordinary moments into something unforgettable, and I am endlessly grateful for that gift.

And the truth is, you didn't become family on your own, you come from it. Linda and Gary raised someone extraordinary, someone who shows up, who loves deeply, and who makes the people around her better just by being in the room. I feel lucky not only to have you, but to be welcomed into the warmth and kindness that defines your entire family.

For Meghan, my best friend across distance and time – no matter how long it has been since we've seen each other, I know you are there, steady in the shadows of my life, reminding me that the deepest friendships need no proof of presence.

For Jill, whom I will always call my sister – you are family, and a connection to my life up north that fills my heart with peace, comfort, and love. For Sheena and Peter, thank you for being everything Alvin and I need in a friendship, for the constant persuasion to write a book, and for using my real-life examples in their own lives.

For Nadia – I will always be grateful that on the very first day of my MBA program, in our economics class, I happened to sit next to you. What started as a simple classroom introduction quickly turned into one of those friendships that feels meant to be. You are the definition of a class act – thoughtful, steady, generous, and endlessly supportive. Through late nights of studying, plenty of laughter, and the shared experience of earning our degrees together, you became far more than a classmate: you became family. I am so thankful our paths crossed that day.

For my brother, Josh, and my sister-in-law, Rachel: Josh, you are more than a brother; you are my companion in laughter, in silly voices, in the endless inside jokes that never get old. Rachel, your grace, kindness, and unwavering support are a gift to our family and proof that love only multiplies when it's shared.

For my sister, Molly, and my brother-in-law, Jason: Molly, you are the spark of joy and mischief that keeps us all laughing, and the reminder that even in life's heaviest moments, humor can be healing. Jason, your steadiness and strength balance this joy with grounding. Together, you have reminded me that family is laughter, loyalty, and love woven together.

For my nieces and nephews: Grace, Andrew, Kash, and Ty. Each of you is a light in my life, a living reminder that the circle continues, and that what we build today is meant to last beyond us. You inspire me to leave behind a legacy that's worthy of you.

I am also deeply grateful for my mother-in-law, Annesta Providence, who we lovingly call "Ma." From the very beginning, she welcomed me with open arms and a generous heart. Her love has never come with conditions, only warmth, kindness, and a quiet strength that holds her entire family together. Through her, I was not only given a mother-in-law, I was given an entire family. To Ma, and to Alvin's wonderful family both near and far, from Trinidad to Canada, thank you for embracing me as one of your own and for surrounding our lives with so much love. Your support, laughter, and presence have meant more than I can ever fully put into words.

For Ellen, a loving force who gracefully pulled me into the world of philanthropy – without your influence, I would not have discovered how persuasion, generosity, and purpose could intersect so powerfully.

For my dream team of editors: Marie and Elizabeth, and Dave. If this book is about the art of the ask, consider this my biggest success story. You said "yes" to the chaos, the passion, the over-commas, the dramatic pauses, and the endless revisions. You persuaded this manuscript into its best, boldest self and somehow did it with grace and humor. I am forever grateful, and possibly emotionally dependent. You all (Adam and Brandon included) are family.

For Mike DeBlasi Swanson, my first "boss" in my fundraising career, who believed in me and my work and made me feel like I was the best fundraiser in the world even though I was just starting out.

For every donor, mentor, and friend who ever said "yes" when it would have been easier to say "no" – your faith changed more than projects or initiatives; it changed me.

For Julianna Marguiles, who welcomed me into her world with open arms – I am so thankful that I had the courage to send you home with my manuscript after meeting for the first time. You have given me so much more than a foreword. You have given me a friendship that I will cherish for the rest of my life. Love you.

And finally, for Joni Mitchell – your music was the soundtrack of my mother's soul, and your letter to me became the inspiration for this very book. Thank you for writing back to me; for giving me words that bridged grief, grace, memory, and possibility. Your letter was more than ink on paper; it was a reminder that daring to ask can summon miracles. Your voice has carried me, your artistry has shaped me, and your song, "The Circle Game," has bound together the love of a mother, the courage of a son, and the message of this book.

And so I leave your words here, as my mother once sang them to me, as the circle continues:

Timothy J. Boynton

Joni Mitchell Called Me Ugly

x

Introduction: My Ask of You

This story begins with a letter from Joni Mitchell. I asked her to sign records for my wedding and she wrote back:

"Your husband is very handsome. You're kind of cute, too."

So, yes, in short, Joni called me ugly. But, keep reading, we'll get to that.

Joni Mitchell Called Me Ugly is not just my story; it's a guide to finding yours. This book is about asking; the kind that transforms relationships, careers, and lives.

In my nearly 20 years in fundraising and development, I've asked for million-dollar gifts, partnerships, and gifts that change skylines, programs, and futures.

Mark Schoenfeld, legendary Broadway writer and producer of *BKLYN: The Musical* and my mentor once called me "monomaniacal," and he wasn't wrong. I had a dream to work on Broadway, and the first chance I got, I moved to New York City.

Mark took a chance on me and allowed me to essentially be his apprentice during *BKLYN*'s Broadway run. I threw myself into it with nothing but obsession, grit, and a floor to sleep on.

That relentless conviction opened doors, taught me how to lead, and ultimately shaped the fundraiser I became: someone who shows up with heart, asks with purpose, and turns belief into action.

I've stood on New York City streets convincing people to buy rush tickets 5 minutes before curtain, and eventually in boardrooms weaving stories that invited people to say "yes" to capital campaigns.

I've stumbled, I've failed, and I've learned that the most powerful tool we have is not perfection, but presence.

Whether you are a fundraiser, a leader, an artist, or simply someone determined to live with more courage, I hope these pages offer you tools, laughter, and the nudge to make your own bold ask. Each chapter gives you a way of thinking about asking, a story to ground it in, and a prompt to help you name what your reason is and what you want to ask for in life.

So, reader, here is my ask of you: walk with me through this journey of finding your courage, your voice, and your next brave question. You never know what doors might open when you dare to ask, even if someone calls you ugly along the way.

I didn't know Joni Mitchell. I had no claim to her time. But I asked anyway. And the answer changed everything.

Note: Throughout this book, you'll hear me use the word "donor". That's the world I've spent my career in, so it's the language that comes most naturally to me. But a good friend of mine, Toanya (who also happens to be one the best entrepreneurs I know), pointed out that not everyone lives in that world, and she's right. So I don't want you to get stuck on that word. Your "donor" might be a client, a customer, a colleague, a boss, an audience, or even someone you love. It's anyone you're asking something of. The principles are the same. The courage is the same. The moment before the ask is always the same. So as you read, feel free to translate. Make it your own. Because this isn't really a book about donors; it's a book about people, and what happens when we have the courage to ask them for something that matters.

Chapter One: The Mothers Who Found Me

By the time I joined Lakeland Regional Health, I was years into living without my mother. The sharpness of grief had softened, and I was fully engaged in my life: dreaming, building, leading, and stepping into work that felt like purpose stitched to calling.

But love leaves a space behind – a room in your heart where light once lived so loudly that its memory still flickers in the quiet.

I wasn't grieving every day. I wasn't lost. I wasn't walking around wounded. But my mother had raised me with such depth, such love, and such unwavering belief that her absence left a stillness inside me – not a void, but a tenderness.

I didn't know it then, but the universe was preparing to send me two women who would continue her work in ways I never could see coming. One arrived with fire. One arrived with grace. Both arrived with purpose.

They would become pillars in my life, not to replace my mother, but to carry her forward through a different doorway.

This is their chapter and this is my gift to them.

Ernestine Tye

Before I ever saw her, I heard about her:

"You're going to ADORE Ernestine."
"She's brilliant. Truly brilliant."

"She'll read you, love you, and roast you all in the same breath." "She will be IMPORTANT to you. Trust me."

I wanted to meet her, so I reached out and she responded immediately. We tried to schedule lunch, but we failed repeatedly and hilariously. It became a mutual bit.

At one point I emailed, "I think the universe is preventing this meeting."

She wrote back, "Honey, when we finally sit down, the world better prepare itself."

Then, one morning, the universe sighed, shrugged, and surrendered. We had the same free hour.

I walked into the restaurant and stopped. There she was. You don't meet Ernestine; you experience Ernestine. She was beautiful, elegant, and poised. Radiating intelligence that hangs in the air like electricity. A woman who carries every room she walks into without lifting a finger.

She stood, arms wide, and said:

"Well, FINALLY. Get over here, sweetheart."

Before I knew what was happening, she cupped my face in both her hands, a gesture so maternal, so intimate, so disarming, and studied me with a depth that felt almost spiritual.

"I knew I'd love you," she said softly. "Soon as I read your first email." And in that moment, I felt it.

A recognition; a familiarity; a feeling that my heart had been waiting for her.

Over lunch, she told me her story, not boastfully, but with the humility of a woman whose life speaks loudly enough for itself:

The first female CFO of one of the largest grocery chains in the South.

She entered male-dominated boardrooms and never asked permission to belong. She broke ceilings while maintaining elegance. She strategized like a general and loved like a mother. She held her own in spaces built to exclude her and made them better by standing there. Her humor was sharp and glorious. Her intelligence was surgical. Her intuition was mystical. Her loyalty was fierce.

But beneath every firestorm of brilliance, there was love – a love that didn't ask questions, a love that didn't hesitate, and a love that wrapped itself around me in an instant, as if her heart recognized mine. At one point she told me: "You needed me. And sweetheart, I think I needed you too."

She was right. I needed her fire. Her truth. Her steadiness. Her humor. Her guidance. Her belief. Her love.

And though she has beautiful children – people she adores profoundly – there was room in her heart for me. True room. Sacred room. Because God sometimes puts two people in each other's paths who were meant to find one another.

Ernestine and I have built an entire secret language out of inside jokes, the kind that would make absolutely no sense to anyone else, and that's precisely what makes them sacred. They're stitched into ordinary moments, whispered in grocery store aisles, exchanged in side-glances across rooms, and signed off in text messages that say everything without saying anything at all. I will not expose them here. Not because I'm being coy, but because some magic is meant to be protected.

Just know this, if you've ever heard us laughing a little too hard or seen us trying to keep a straight face at the most inappropriate moment, you'd understand. And if you've ever heard me say, with equal parts judgement and love, "You ought to be ashamed," you would know without having to ask, that it's not criticism at all, it's the form of affection in our peculiar and perfect vocabulary.

She didn't replace my mother. She continued her. In her own brilliant, fierce, unforgettable way. And I need her to know this, clearly, deeply, and forever:

Ernestine, you are one of the greatest loves of my life. You are the mother of my adulthood. You are a blessing I thank God for every single day. And loving you, being loved by you, has changed me in ways you will never fully know.

Sarah McKay

Where Ernestine arrived like fire, Sarah McKay arrived like sunlight: warm, gentle, and gracious. She was a true southern belle, beautiful inside and out, with a presence that made every room softer.

She invited me to her home for our first meeting; a gesture that told me immediately that this was intimacy, not formality. Her house welcomed me like a warm embrace.

Photos were everywhere. Stories on the walls. Memory and meaning in every corner. We sat at her kitchen table, the throne of a southern matriarch, and I explained our hospital's hopes and needs.

She listened with the kind of attention that feels like love. "Well darling," she said, "if you care about it, that's all I need to hear."

That was Sarah. Pure belief. Pure trust. Pure heart.

And then came the moment that sealed her in my life forever.

At one of the first events my husband Alvin attended, with a room full of community leaders, he looked up and saw Sarah rise from the head table, gripping her cane, eyes locked on him.

"Tim," he whispered urgently, "She's coming toward me. Is everything okay?" She approached with purpose, cane tapping in slow determination.

Alvin froze.

Sarah reached him. Stopped. Dropped her cane. And wrapped him in a hug so fierce it dissolved every fear.

"Honey," she whispered in her warm southern drawl, "I already love you. Because I love him," and she pointed at me.

It was unconditional acceptance. Immediate. Complete. Sacred.

Sarah has since passed. But the love she gave me – and the love she gave Alvin – lives in me with a permanence I cannot explain.

She mothered with grace, ease, and tenderness, and a love that asks nothing in return. I still keep in touch with her family because they welcomed me with open arms, just as she had. I loved Sarah. And I miss her every day.

Joni Mitchell Called Me Ugly

Chapter Two: Me and Joni

If you had told me fifteen years ago that I'd be on a first-name basis with Joni Mitchell, I would've laughed. Not because it felt impossible, but because it felt too sacred.

Joni was my mother's north star. Her voice wasn't background noise in our home; it was oxygen. It wrapped around us during Sunday morning breakfast, floating around a sun-lit kitchen while my mom swayed at the stove, singing along softly, but never over Joni. She knew better.

When I lost my mom, I was 29. At that age, I didn't know how to grieve her death so I held on tightly, almost denying her absence. I clung onto anything that carried even a hint of her: vinyl records, phrases she used, the way she'd hum that one line from "The Circle Game." I held on for dear life.

I missed my mom, and I still do. I also still grieve for the moments she missed in my life. My first promotion, my MBA ceremony, and my wedding day.

Like many engaged couples in 2020, my fiancé, Alvin, and I were piecing together cancelled wedding plans due to the pandemic. We ultimately decided to elope on the beach with only a handful of our closest family.

As the day approached, so did the ache of wanting my mom there. So, I decided to ask for something that felt impossible: I wanted to ask Joni Mitchell to be part of my wedding. I wanted to ask her to sign my mom's records as gifts for my wedding party.

People told me I was crazy, and you may be thinking the same. Not only was Joni's name so sacred to me, but she's nearly untouchable as a legendary music icon. This was also before she made her incredible return to the stage at the Newport Folk Festival in 2022. In other words, my odds were slim to none.

But reader, I need you to suspend your preconceived notions of possibilities. This book, if anything, is my way of inviting you to imagine what would happen if you were bold enough to just ask.

This is the first example of many that I will share with you about how amazing things can happen when you have the conviction, the courage, and the vulnerability to ask for what you want. I promise you'll learn something about yourself that may surprise you and inspire you to be more bold in your life. If anything, you can laugh at my delusion and watch it pay off.

It started the way all bold asks begin: with a single thread. I pulled on it. Then another. And another. Six degrees of separation turned into six phone calls, a few favors, a whole lot of charm, and the one thing that makes any ask powerful: a reason that matters.

I asked her to sign records for our wedding party in my mom's memory. She said yes.

She asked for photos of me, my family, and my fiancé. She asked if I would be willing to tell her our story. She signed the records and even wrote a letter back.

In the letter, she said my husband was "very handsome." And me? She wrote that I was "kind of cute too."

Now, listen, I don't know how many people in this world have been backhandedly complimented by a musical icon, but I'm one of them. It was the most poetic insult I've ever received.

That letter didn't just honor my mother; it changed me. It reminded me of the power of asking, of reaching out heart-first with nothing but faith and a story. It was also the spark that ignited what you're holding in your hands right now.

And since that day, I've jokingly told people, "Joni and I are close now." We don't text (yet). We don't have brunch (yet). Sure, I think about her more than she thinks about me, but that's how 95% of friendships work anyway. Still, we're connected. Not just because she said yes, but because I dared to ask.

So yes, Joni Mitchell may have called me ugly, but I'm choosing to believe she saw something in me worth responding to.

The takeaway: Asking is an act of hope.

Asking is more than a question; it's an act of vulnerability, hope, and vision. The power of a great ask lies not in how it's phrased, but in how deeply you believe in why you're making it. People respond to authenticity, not polish.

Chapter Two: Journal Prompt

What would you ask if you knew they'd say yes?

Think of something you've been afraid to ask for professionally or personally, and reflect on the following questions:

- What's holding you back?

- What would it mean if they said yes?

- Why do you believe this ask matters?

- What story would help someone understand why you're asking?

Now, write the ask. Make it bold. Make it heartfelt. Practice believing it.

Chapter Three: Curtain Call to Capital Campaigns

When I lost my mom in 2009 to cancer, I'd seen what compassion looked like through her caregivers. I was moved by them, and I realized I wanted to dedicate my life to giving back in that same way—through healthcare.

Although I ultimately left my Broadway career behind to enter the world of healthcare philanthropy, I did take away life-changing lessons from my time under the lights. I learned that timing is everything. That energy matters. That no one follows a flat note. And most of all, I learned that people want to be moved.

Fundraising works for the same reason great theater works: people respond to honesty, conviction, and the courage to create a moment that moves them. A successful ask is not about the pitch, but the person behind it: steady, sincere, and willing to make space for someone else to believe.

The first time I made a real solicitation, I panicked. Creating an emotional moment across a dinner table felt nothing like waiting for applause, and the silence felt brutal.

So I reached for the one place I felt steady: the theater. I imagined the donor as my scene partner, the mission as my script, and the moment as mine to shape.

And it worked.

I told the story, let the pauses land, read the room, and delivered the ask. The donor said yes.

This is how it happened:

My first real ask happened in a small, windowless office at a community hospital in New Hampshire. Picture beige walls, an overstuffed filing cabinet, the lingering smell of disinfectant and burnt coffee, and fluorescent lights that hummed like they had something to say.

I was new, and a little too eager. I rehearsed every sentence in the mirror the night before, pacing my apartment like I was preparing for a monologue.

The donor was a retired local businessman. He was kind and quiet and sat across from me with his hands folded like he was waiting for something. Not a pitch. Not a performance. Something real.

I talked about the hospital, the need, the project, the lives that would be touched, and I watched him closely. I searched his face for hints. Was I saying too much? Not enough? Was I losing him?

Then, without ceremony or flourish, I asked:

"Would you consider a gift of ten thousand dollars?"

A beat followed long enough to feel like it might never end. He nodded.

"Yes," he said. "I think we can do that."

I froze. In that instant, I realized he wasn't just saying yes to a number. He was saying yes to me, my belief, my conviction, and the possibility I had laid in front of him.

I walked out of that meeting feeling like I had just raised the moon out of the ocean. Ten thousand dollars felt like a miracle.

I learned that day that a gift is never just a financial decision, but an emotional, personal, and deeply vulnerable one.

The takeaway: Don't be perfect, be vulnerable.

Fundraising is not about perfection; it's about presence. Every ask is a live performance: you walk in, read the room, adjust your timing, and speak from the heart. The goal isn't to dazzle; it's to connect. People say yes when they trust that you truly believe.

Chapter Three: Journal Prompt

What stage are you standing on?

Think of a time when you were fully "in the moment."

- When do you feel most confident sharing your ideas or inviting people to join your cause?

- What stories do you tell over and over again?

- How do you prepare for big moments? What rituals get you ready?

- Where in your work do you need to step into the spotlight more boldly?

Chapter Four: Conviction Sells

When I first started fundraising, I thought the secret was in the pitch and the carefully designed deck with all the colorful charts. While those things matter, I quickly learned that no one says yes because of a PowerPoint slide. They say yes because of conviction.

Conviction is the difference between presenting an idea and embodying it. Conviction is contagious.

I saw this in my Broadway days. I'd watch actors audition with flawless technique, perfect notes, and memorized lines, but something would fall flat. Then another actor would walk in, a little rough around the edges, but they believed every word, every gesture, and every breath of their performance.

Suddenly, the room leaned forward. That's conviction.

Fundraising works the same way. People don't give to polished perfection; they give to authentic conviction.

I once sat across from a donor who told me, "Tim, I can tell when someone is selling me. I can also tell when someone is living what they're asking for." Conviction isn't something you can fake. You either have it or you don't. And when you do, people feel it.

Conviction is also what gives you staying power. There will always be skeptics and someone ready to poke holes in your vision, or to challenge your numbers and ask, "Why you? Why now? Why this?"

Without conviction, those questions rattle you. With it, they sharpen you.

I've walked into rooms where I was the youngest person at the table. Yet I've walked out with commitments that no one thought possible. Not because I was the smartest, but because I was the surest. My conviction filled the gaps my résumé couldn't.

Conviction isn't arrogance or bulldozing over doubt. It's holding your vision so clearly and passionately that others can lean on your conviction until they make it their own.

There was a donor who came into my life early in my career. Not a headline donor, just a quiet, steady presence. She made modest annual gifts. Ones that were recorded in the system, acknowledged with a thank-you letter, and filed neatly away.

She never asked for recognition, never sought the spotlight, never wanted her name in a brochure or etched in glass. When she gave, she gave privately, almost shyly as if the act itself was more meaningful when it remained unseen.

However, there was something about her; something in her questions, and in the way she listened and watched.

Quiet donors are rarely small donors.

Sometimes they're just waiting to see who means what they say. So I didn't ask her for more.

I didn't push.

I didn't hurry.

I simply stayed present.

Over time, we had coffee, talked about books, her garden, and her grandchildren. She loved hydrangeas because they "change color depending on what they grow from."

She said it casually, but I heard it loudly. People change the same way.

A year passed, then two, then five.

Through those years, I never treated her like a small donor, because she wasn't.

She was a believer in progress.

Belief that was slow, steady, and earned.

One afternoon, she asked if she could take a tour of the hospital. Not the usual, scripted version where shiny new lobbies and perfectly placed picture frames lined the hall.

She wanted to see the in-between places where humanity lived. So I showed her.

We walked through hallways that never make brochures. Past families trying to be brave.

Past nurses holding the emotional weight of rooms that needed more than medicine.

Past the quiet spaces where love and fear sit side by side.

She didn't say much, and at the end of the tour, she stood still for a long time. Then she turned to me and said, "This matters, doesn't it?"

Not as a question, but as a realization.

"Yes," I said. "It matters more than anything." And she nodded, almost to herself.

Months later, she scheduled a meeting. As we sat in my office, the afternoon light poured in slanted through the blinds.

She had a plain, manila folder on the table with her name on the tab. Inside was her estate plan.

She had chosen the hospital as one of her primary legacy beneficiaries. A gift many, many times larger than anything she had ever given in life.

She looked at me and said, "I didn't need to see a proposal. I needed to see you live the mission you claim to believe in."

And I understood.

Conviction sells.

Not because it convinces, but because it offers something solid to lean on. Her small annual gifts were never small. They were steps.

She was watching to see if I would keep showing up long after the campaign banners came down and the presentations ended.

She was looking for constancy and sincerity. For a mission lived, not pitched.

And when she found it, she didn't give more; she gave a legacy.

Conviction doesn't just earn buy-in from donors, it earns buy-in from teams, boards, and colleagues. They want to attach themselves to a vision that feels unshakable, even when the path isn't clear. When you show up with that kind of energy, people don't just buy in, they lean in.

One of my favorite examples of this came from a campaign meeting where we were discussing an ambitious naming opportunity. The numbers were big and the stakes were bigger. People in the room were nervous, hesitant, and almost apologetic about the size of the ask. I stopped the conversation and said: "If we don't believe this is possible, how can we expect anyone else to?"

You cannot ask a community to care about something your own team treats like a line item.

So, we built a culture of philanthropy.

We stopped talking about fundraising as an obligation and started talking about it as belonging. We taught nurses, technicians, board members, and executives how to tell the story of why this work matters.

We stopped focusing on dollars raised and started focusing on hearts engaged.

The takeaway: Believe in what and *why* you're asking.

The most compelling ask isn't the one with the perfect pitch; it's the one backed by unshakable belief. Conviction bridges doubt, inspires trust, and makes the impossible feel inevitable.

Chapter Four: Journal Prompt

Where does your conviction show?

- Think about a time you convinced someone of something big. What belief carried you through?

- When have you felt like, "I've got this in the bag?" What was it and why did you feel so sure?

- What would your work look like if you leaned into conviction more and polish less?

- Who in your life embodies conviction and how can you learn from them?

Chapter Five: Public Speaking & Presence

Some say they fear public speaking more than death. I've never been one of them.

I wasn't born a natural speaker – far from it. I have, however, always had stage presence.

I learned this watching the actors from the wings during *BKLYN*'s Broadway run. When you perform, you don't just deliver lines, you embody them. The same is true in public speaking. The content matters, but the presence behind it matters more.

We've all watched someone say all the right words with none of the weight. The delivery was flat, the body language unsure, and the eye contact was scattered. You walked away unimpressed and maybe unsure what they were even trying to say.

And then there are the speeches you remember. Not because they were perfect – often they weren't – but because the speaker carried real conviction. Even if they stumbled, they held the room through belief, energy, and presence.

One of my most memorable moments at the podium was at a campaign kickoff event. I started my speech with the story of a single patient whose life had been changed at our hospital.

I paused. I looked people in the eye. When I finished, there was silence for a moment; not because I'd lost them, but because I had them. And then the applause came.

The numbers were daunting, the stakes enormous. I could have leaned on charts and statistics, but instead I chose to connect with the audience.

This can be applied to every human interaction you have at work, at home, and in life. Remember:

- Your body speaks first. People read your confidence, energy, and openness before you ever open your mouth.

- Silence persuades. A well-placed pause lands deeper than a rushed sentence.

- Vulnerability connects. Honest moments of fear, failure, or sacrifice draw people closer, not away.

- Energy is contagious. Your belief fuels the room; your boredom drains the room; your passion lifts the room.

Your presence lives in the smallest details, and mastering those details takes time. When you step into leadership, how you show up in meetings, at events, and in the community is observed more closely than you realize.

I call this executive-level presence. And it took me a while to earn mine.

Developing presence requires a willingness to be perceived. And when people perceive you – especially mentors – you will receive feedback that may sting but ultimately serves you.

I remember sitting at the conference table outside my CEO's office. Neutral walls, too many awards, unforgiving lighting that made me wish I had slept more the night before. I was younger and still figuring out who I was as a leader.

At that time, my wardrobe consisted of what I could afford, not what reflected the leader I was becoming. My dress shirts were always a little too tight in the collar, so I never closed the top button. I would leave it undone and pretend it was intentional. Almost a casual, artistic flair, like a remnant of "Broadway me" trying to survive in a boardroom.

I told myself no one noticed. People always notice.

My CEO sat down, looked at me, and said, "Tim. If you are going to lead here, you need to buy shirts that fit."

The words hit like a slap.

I wanted to sink into the floor, or at the very least run to a tailor immediately. I wanted to defend myself. To explain that I was still adjusting and that I would get there.

But I didn't say anything.

I knew she wasn't talking about fabric; she was talking about identity.

She was telling me that leadership is not just what you say, it's how you show up in the world.

It was harsh, uncomfortable, and exactly what I needed.

That afternoon I bought one shirt. Just one. It cost more than I wanted to spend, and the salesperson told me my posture improved the moment I put it on. I laughed, but she was right.

I didn't just look different; I felt different.

The shirt mattered not because it was nicer, but because I chose it. I chose to step into the role I was growing into instead of clinging to the one I had outgrown.

Presence is showing up for the room, for the mission, and most importantly, for yourself.

In fundraising, you're asking people to trust you with their resources and their values. You become the face of the cause, not metaphorically, but literally.

I learned this during a campaign kickoff where I addressed a room of leaders, donors, physicians, and partners. The energy was cautious. They weren't evaluating numbers; they were evaluating me.

They needed assurance.

So I didn't open with data or timelines. I began with stillness.

I let the room settle.

I let the moment breathe.

Then I spoke slowly, deliberately, not to impress them, but to include them. Because presence is not dominance, it's invitation.

People may be drawn to charisma, but they trust certainty; quiet, grounded certainty shaped by experience, responsibility, and purpose.

Over time, the work itself taught me how to hold that certainty. It shaped me, matured me, refined me. And I became the kind of leader people could place confidence in.

Public speaking is not performance; it's embodiment. When you stand before a room, you are the physical expression of what you're asking others to believe is possible.

The takeaway: Presence persuades more than words.

The most persuasive speakers aren't the most polished; they're the most real. What moves audiences is not flawless delivery, but the honesty and certainty they feel standing in front of them.

Chapter Five: Journal Prompt

Where does your presence shine?

- Think of a time you spoke and truly moved people. What made it work?

- Where do you hold back in your speaking or presence, and why?

- What role does vulnerability play in how you communicate?

- How can you practice presence; not just in speeches, but in every conversation?

Chapter Six: Branding Yourself

When you hear the word "brand," what comes to mind? Consider iconic logos like Coca-Cola, McDonald's, and Nike. And slogans like "Just Do It" and "I'm Lovin' It" redefined the way people respond to products.

With their recognizable brands they sell not just a drink or a shoe, they're creating a reaction, a feeling, a nostalgia, and an experience. They rely on human emotion and connection to push their product forward.

Creating a personal brand for yourself is not too different; just fewer logos.

In the last chapter I shared my thoughts on how your presence in a moment can affect your ask. Similarly, but on a deeper level, cultivating your brand can take time. Your brand should be the way you want others to remember you, how you want them to feel when you leave the room, and how they trust the consistency of your message.

The best fundraisers, leaders, and communicators understand this. They don't just "have" a brand; they steward it over time. They make sure their words, actions, and presence align.

One of the most powerful parts of branding is consistency. People trust what they can predict. If you show up differently every time – scattered, inconsistent, or unclear – people hesitate. But when your brand is steady, trust will grow.

Branding is also about authenticity. If your brand is a mask, people will sense it. But when it's an honest reflection of who you are, your brand becomes your most persuasive asset. It tells the world: "This is who I am, and this is what you can count on from me."

Branding yourself is not about image. It's not about logos or taglines or curated phrases. Branding yourself is about deciding what story your life is telling and then living that story with enough clarity that others recognize it.

When I began speaking publicly about this book, I was not just promoting a project. I was revealing a philosophy, a way of being, a way of leading, a way of asking, a way of connecting purpose to presence.

So I had to ask myself, "When people hear my name, what do I want them to *feel*? Not think, but *feel*."

Your brand is the emotional signature you leave in a room once you walk out of it.

Branding yourself is not an act of self-promotion.

It's an act of self-alignment where you decide who you are, you live it consistently, and the world learns how to recognize you.

The takeaway: Your brand is always persuading.

Your brand speaks before you do. Make sure it tells the story you want people to believe.

Chapter Six: Journal Prompt

Who do you want to start or continue shaping your brand?

- What three words would people use to describe your brand today?

- Do those words match the story you want to tell?

- Where is your brand inconsistent with your true self?

- What small action could you take this week to align your brand with your values?

32

Chapter Seven: Storytelling is Strategy

I've been in countless boardrooms where the data was airtight, the financial models flawless, the logic undeniable, and still, the answer was no.

Why?

Because people aren't persuaded by numbers alone. They're persuaded by stories.

A story is the oldest persuasion tool we have. Long before there were spreadsheets or pitch decks, there were stories around campfires. Stories are how humans make sense of risk, hope, and sacrifice. They don't just transfer information; they transfer emotion. And emotion moves people to act.

I learned this lesson on Broadway. Every great show lives or dies on its story. You can have the best costumes, the biggest sets, the most technically brilliant performers, but if the story doesn't land, the audience won't stay with you.

I remember one donor meeting that could have gone either way. On paper, the project was strong. We had all the facts lined up, the case for support was bulletproof. But as the conversation went on, I could feel their interest fading.

So, I shifted. I stopped talking about square footage and start-up costs. Instead, I told the story of a single patient whose life had been saved by a similar program. I painted a picture of what would have happened if that patient hadn't had access to care. I described the moment the family realized they'd been given more time.

The donor's eyes softened. They leaned forward. And in that moment, I knew: the facts hadn't persuaded them; the story had.

Storytelling isn't decoration; it's strategy. It frames the ask. It sets the stage, creating urgency and resonance. Without it, you're just trading information. With it, you're creating connections.

Here's the key: persuasion lives in the intersection of story and strategy. A good story without strategy is entertainment. Strategy without story is cold. But when you bring them together, you create an actionable impact.

And stories don't just persuade donors; they persuade teams, boards, and even ourselves. The most powerful stories are simple, specific, and human. They don't overwhelm with details; they invite people to feel. They don't aim for perfection; they aim for connection. They don't lecture; they linger.

There was a young mother who came to our hospital in the middle of the night.

Her body was failing. Her spirit had been stretched thin long before the ambulance arrived. By the time she reached our doors, she had nearly died.

The ICU was quiet except for the steady rhythm of machines breathing for her while her body tried to remember how.

Her husband sat beside her bed every single day. He did not leave.

He held her hand, even when it did not squeeze back. He told her about their daughter at home. About the way she insisted on picking out her own clothes. About how she asked every night when Mommy was coming home.

Weeks passed. And then one morning, she opened her eyes. Not dramatically. Not like a movie scene with gasps and applause. Just a blink. A slow return. A quiet decision to stay.

When I tell this story to donors, I don't start with ventilators or staffing ratios or clinical complexity. I don't talk about technology.

I talk about the chair. The chair her husband refused to leave.

Because that chair represents everything.

It represents hope that refuses to clock out. It represents a health system strong enough to hold space for miracles, even the quiet ones. It represents a family that did not have to plan a funeral.

We're not raising money for machines.

We're raising money so that someone can sit in that chair and believe their person will come back.

At a donor event not long ago, I shared another ICU story.

It was about a retired executive who had suffered a massive cardiac event. He arrived unconscious. His adult daughter flew in from out of state and took up residence in that same kind of chair.

She brought her laptop and worked remotely from his bedside. She slept in thirty-minute increments. She memorized the rhythm of the monitors. She learned the names of every nurse on the rotation.

Every day, before leaving the unit to shower, she leaned close to her father and said the same thing.

"I'm not going anywhere."

After the event, a donor approached me.

He told me about his own brother who had spent weeks in an ICU years earlier. He described the smell of antiseptics. The constant hum. The helplessness of standing there while professionals fought a battle he could not.

"I remember the chair," he said.

He made a gift the next morning.

Not because I cornered him.

Not because I showed him a campaign goal.

Not because I perfected the pitch.

But because he saw himself.

In fundraising, you aren't simply telling a story. You're building a doorway. You're creating a place where someone can recognize their own love, their own fear, or their own hope.

When they see themselves inside the story, the ask no longer feels like a transaction.

It feels like alignment.

You don't persuade by pushing.

You persuade by inviting.

And when someone realizes their gift is not about equipment, but about protecting moments, protecting families, protecting that chair that becomes sacred in the hardest hours of someone's life, the decision becomes clear.

The best fundraising does not convince.

It connects.

In fundraising, you don't just tell the story. You hand someone the pen and invite them to write themselves into it. You give them a role: hero, partner, champion. And once they see themselves inside the story, the ask is no longer about you. It's about them.

The takeaway: Strategy without story doesn't stick.

Persuasion doesn't come from facts or logic alone; it comes from story. A story makes the ask real, urgent, and personal. It turns information into invitation.

Chapter Seven: Journal Prompt

What story are you telling?

- What's one story that illustrates your mission better than any statistic?

- How can you frame your ask so the other person sees themselves inside it?

- When have you been persuaded by a story rather than data?

- What story do you tell yourself that fuels your own conviction?

Chapter Eight: The Cultivation Dance

Fundraising is often described as a science; a formula of numbers, networks, and projections.

But I see it as a dance.

Like any great dance, it's about rhythm, timing, and trust. You do not rush onto the floor, grab someone's hand, and demand they move with you. You invite. You lead gently. You match their pace. You listen. You move together.

People tend to think persuasion happens during the ask; you walk into a room, deliver the perfect line, and the donor says yes. But persuasion begins long before that. It lives in the coffee meetings, the handwritten notes, the hallway conversations where you show someone they matter.

Cultivation is rarely dramatic. It's quiet, patient work. The kind that never shows up in campaign reports or board slide decks. It's not about urging someone to move faster. It's about learning how to move with them.

There was a donor I worked with early on who taught me this lesson.

He was brilliant and disciplined. He was someone who planned his life in seasons rather than days. If you rushed him, you lost him. If you tried to impress him, he retreated. He could see through intention the way light passes through clear water.

At our first meeting, I arrived prepared: a polished case for support, projected outcomes, a crisp vision. He listened politely, but his eyes stayed distant, as though measuring me.

When we stood to leave, he said, "You care deeply, and I respect that. But you're not talking *to* me. You're talking *at* me."

Earlier in my career, that would have stung. This time, it guided me. I stopped pitching and started listening.

I asked about his work, his family, his beliefs, his hesitations. I watched what brightened his face and what dimmed it. I noticed the pauses before certain answers, the subjects he returned to, the way he spoke about legacy as something earned, not claimed.

Months passed. Philanthropy came up only occasionally. Mostly, we talked about the economy, the strength of oak trees, and how grief reshapes a person but doesn't diminish their capacity to love.

Gradually, he let me match his pace. One afternoon he said, "Walk with me."

We circled the perimeter of his property in near silence; no pitch, no agenda, just presence. The winter leaves were thinning, and the light was low. When we finished, he said, "I think I understand now why this matters to you."

He didn't say yes that day, but something shifted.

When the yes finally came, it felt inevitable not because I persuaded him, but because we arrived there together. I didn't lead. I followed. And when the moment was right, we moved in step.

When someone says yes in this way, they aren't saying yes to an organization or proposal. They're saying yes to belonging, to meaning, to the version of themselves revealed in the act of giving.

That's persuasion at its most dignified; the moment when the dance becomes mutual, and both partners understand why they're moving.

The takeaway: Cultivation is persuasion in slow motion.

Persuasion doesn't begin at the ask. It begins in every small interaction where trust is built. Cultivation is about rhythm, patience, and presence. The ask is simply the next step in a dance already underway.

And like in any dance, you will misread the tempo or move ahead of the music. What matters is not the stumble, but how gracefully you return to the rhythm.

Chapter Eight: Journal Prompt

How do you dance in relationships?

- Think of a donor or partner you've been "dancing" with. What's the rhythm of that relationship?

- Where have you rushed the steps? Where have you been patient?

- How do you show people you value them outside of the ask?

- What's one small, intentional step you could take this week to move the dance forward?

Chapter Nine: Turning No into Maybe

The first time I heard *no* from a donor, I smiled, nodded, and left the meeting with a pit in my stomach. I blew it, I thought. I replayed every moment like a director watching dailies; pausing at my stumbles and dissecting every word.

No has taught me more than *yes* ever has. In theater, if an audience isn't responding, you don't walk off stage. You adjust, shift your timing, find new energy, and try something different next time.

Fundraising is no different.

No can also mean *not yet* or *not this way* or *prove to me why I should care*. I learned this from Mark Schoenfeld. He was full of *nos* in the beginning.

No, you can't sit in on that meeting.

No, I don't want you hanging out with the producers. No, this is above your pay grade.

Each time, I responded intentionally and persistently with a reason, story, and a different angle of why it should be yes.

Eventually, I convinced him. Not because he gave in, but because we finally aligned.

Real persuasion isn't about pressure; it's about alignment. People don't say yes to information; they say yes to emotion, trust, feeling understood, and seeing their values reflected in the ask. I've had donors tell me no and return six months later with a yes (sometimes an even bigger one).

By now, you may have guessed that I love theater imagery. And what is theater without choreography?

No is part of the choreography of your ask. It gives the ask its rhythm, keeps you on your toes, and is essential to keeping the plot moving.

So when someone tells me no, I don't flinch. I listen. I pause. I come back smarter and softer. Because behind every *no* is the most powerful word in fundraising: *maybe.* And *maybe* is where the magic lives.

From that *maybe*, you start asking:

- What would need to change for this to feel right?

- Is it the timing, or the vision?

- What is truly at stake?

One of my donors, Andrew, was not an easy ask. Not because he was difficult. He was principled and knew exactly what he cared about. Even more importantly, he knew what he did not care about.

His philanthropy went almost entirely to the welfare of animals. He funded rescues, sanctuaries, transport programs, rehabilitation, and work. If it had fur or feathers or a name that sounded like something you would find in a meadow, Andrew was behind it. He believed animals offered a purity that humans did not.

So when I first approached him about supporting healthcare, I already knew the answer.

He listened politely, nodded with kindness, and said, "It's a worthy cause, Tim, truly. But my heart belongs to the animals." The tone was final. He was not shutting the door. He was simply telling the truth. There was no room to push. If I had, the relationship would have ended before it ever began.

So, I did not push.

I stayed. I learned. I listened. I asked him questions about the animals he helped. I learned their names. I visited the rescue barn he supported. I went into his world before asking him to step into mine.

Over time, we became friends.

Not surface level friends, but real ones. The kind where conversations have long pauses because neither of you is in a hurry to fill them, and a cup of coffee lasts a few hours.

One afternoon, I invited him to visit the hospital. No fundraising pitch. No appointment on the books. Just a walk. I showed him the pediatric unit. The family waiting rooms. The quiet spaces where decisions shaped futures. We didn't talk about money. We talked about why healing requires community.

Something softened in him that day.

Not dramatically. Just perceptibly, like the way snow begins to melt first where the light shines.

Months passed, and we continued to talk. We talked about the weight of being responsible for something that's bigger than yourself.

"Animals cannot speak," he said. "That's why I speak for them."

I said, "You're right. And there are people who have lost the ability to speak for themselves too."

He understood.

So when he walked into my office that day, I had no sense of what was coming. He was carrying a small, unassuming black gym bag, the kind you could buy at any sporting goods store. He set it gently on the chair across from me.

He sat down. Took a breath. Looked at me for a very long moment, and said, "I think I want to help."

I nodded. I let him lead. He unzipped the bag.

Inside were gold bars.

Real ones. Heavy, cold, neatly stacked, and quiet in their weight. The kind of quiet that means something monumental has entered the room.

"I do not believe money should sit still," he said. "I believe it should move toward meaning."

I felt my throat tighten.

I knew what this gift represented.

This was not a change in financial priority. This was a change in identity, a widening, and a reorientation of where his love could live.

He said yes, not because I pressured him. He said yes because we shared space. Trust grew in quiet moments.

We turned no into yes together, proving that no is not a rejection, it's an opportunity.

This opportunity is a signal: it's time to understand your donor more deeply and gain their trust.

When you do, the yes that follows may not just open wallets; it may open worlds.

The takeaway: *No* is an opportunity, not an ending.

This rejection is not as personal, but directional. Every *no* teaches you something about the person, the timing, the delivery, or even yourself. If you stay curious instead of crushed, you'll uncover what's behind it and find your way back with more clarity.

Persistence isn't pushing. It's presence over time. Your job isn't to force a yes. It's to stay in the room long enough to earn one.

Chapter Nine: Journal Prompt

What's behind the no?

Think back to a time when someone told you *no*. Revisit the moment without judgment. Then explore:

- What did the *no* actually mean?

- Were you clear about the ask, or was there room for uncertainty?

- How did you respond emotionally?

- What would you do differently now?

- Have you ever said *no* to someone else? Why?

- What would it look like to ask again differently?

Chapter Ten: Every Ask Has a Cost

There's a myth people love to tell about success: it comes from talent, luck, or being in the right place at the right time. And sure, those things help, but anyone who has ever built something that mattered knows the truth: success is built on sacrifice.

Sacrifice isn't glamorous. It doesn't sparkle like a standing ovation or shine like a ribbon-cutting ceremony. It's quiet, gritty, and often invisible.

It's the late nights, the early mornings, the missed weekends, and the constant trade-offs that no one applauds. Sacrifice doesn't make headlines, but it shapes destinies.

I've learned that sacrifice is the true currency of a meaningful life.

When I was nineteen and moved to New York, I didn't have money for furniture. I had an air mattress that kept deflating at 3:00AM every night. I'd wake up on the hardwood floor with my back aching, but I stayed.

I sacrificed comfort for proximity to opportunity. In those sleepless nights, I learned that the very thing you give up becomes the ground you stand on later. Sometimes you must give up things in order to thrive forward. Success doesn't always come easy.

Later, in fundraising, sacrifice looked different. It wasn't about sleeping on floors. It was about turning down short-term wins for long-term relationships; choosing not to chase the easy donor dollars because I believed in cultivating something bigger, deeper, and more meaningful; saying no to personal recognition so that others could shine.

Sacrifice also showed up in unexpected places. Like when I realized leadership sometimes meant stepping back so someone else could step forward. That's a different kind of sacrifice, the surrender of ego. And it's one of the hardest.

The truth is, every ask has sacrifice built into it. When you ask someone to give, you're really asking them to trade one thing for another: money for mission, time for impact, comfort for change. The job of a fundraiser isn't to pretend that sacrifice doesn't exist; it's to show that the trade is worth it.

I once met with a donor who looked me dead in the eye and said, "Tim, you know I could spend this money on a vacation house. Convince me why this matters more." He wasn't joking. He was testing me. I realized he was asking a question we all wrestle with: is what I'm giving up worth what I'm gaining?

However, when your values are clear, giving something up doesn't feel like deprivation, it feels like purpose.

Sacrifice is why people give away fortunes instead of hoarding them. It's why artists pour themselves into work with no guarantees. It's why parents go hungry so their children can eat. It's why communities rise after tragedy, offering time, money, and energy when it would be easier to turn away.

Sacrifice is the soil. Growth is the harvest.

The takeaway: Sacrifice is the price of meaning.

True sacrifice doesn't remove things; it makes space for something greater.

Chapter Ten: Journal Prompt

What are you willing to trade?

- What's one comfort, habit, or luxury you've already given up to pursue your calling?

- What's something you're still holding onto that might be limiting your growth?

- If someone asked you, "Convince me why this matters more," what would you say?

- Can you identify a time when sacrifice felt like a loss, and a time when it felt like purpose?

52

Chapter Eleven: The Anatomy of a Big Ask

Every fundraiser knows "the moment." The air shifts. The conversation slows. The anticipation builds. And then, it's time for the ask.

I've made asks in boardrooms with sweeping city views, at kitchen tables with coffee still brewing, and even on the side of a hockey rink. The settings change, but the anatomy of an ask stays the same.

- The Foundation: Relationship/Trust

- The Heartbeat: Story

- The Muscles: Conviction

- The Breath: Silence

- The Hands: Invitation

I will never forget one donor who looked at me after I made a very bold ask, one far larger than anyone expected them to consider. He smiled and said, "You know what I love about you, Tim? You ask me for things that scare me a little, but you make me want to say yes."

That's persuasion at its finest. Not manipulation. Not pressure. An invitation that feels aligned and purposeful, so the yes becomes the only answer that makes sense.

And sometimes the donor does not say yes. Not yet. But if the anatomy is strong, even a no becomes fertile ground for the future.

Before I began fundraising, I assumed the biggest asks happened in boardrooms. Long tables. Leather chairs. Water pitchers lined up with quiet formality.

But one of the most meaningful asks, and one of the most significant gifts I ever received, happened nowhere near a conference room.

It happened at a hockey game.

The arena was freezing and loud in the way only rinks can be. Fans shouting. Skates cutting across the ice. The sharp echo of metal on cold air. I stood near the glass with a donor's wife, not in a curated moment, just two people watching the world move fast.

I had known her and her family for years. We shared meals, traded stories, talked about family and worry and hope. We were not discussing philanthropy that day. We were simply standing in the arena, cheering and snacking on popcorn.

As she watched the players skate harder, faster, fighting to stay upright, she said quietly, almost to herself, "It's a lot to watch the people you love go through things you cannot control."

She was not talking about hockey.

I looked at her and did not fill the silence. I let it settle. After a long moment she said, "Tell me again about the program you are building. The one for families and behavioral wellness. The one that makes sure no one goes through things alone."

She was ready. Not because I asked her, but because the moment made space for it.

So I told her. Not with statistics or polished talking points. I spoke the way you speak to someone you care about. Clear. Honest. Without trying to convince.

Her eyes stayed fixed on the ice. "We can help with that," she said. Not a question, but recognition.

By the end of the week, she and her husband committed a gift so significant it reshaped our entire project. Later that year when her husband was getting an award for his philanthropy, he ended his acceptance speech with, "Never let Tim Boynton sit next to your wife at a hockey game!"

The room spilled into laughter. This is the same donor who once said, "You know Tim is a good fundraiser when he asks me to lunch and I actually want to go."

It was the best compliment I have ever received. He was not saying, "he convinced me." He was saying, "he made me feel seen."

That's the heart of persuasion. It happens in every moment before the big ask. The laughter. The quiet. The trust. The willingness to stand beside someone in the cold when there is no script.

People do not say yes because of information. They say yes because they recognize themselves in the story you are inviting them into.

This gift did not come from strategy. It came from trust, story, conviction, silence, and a silent invitation to allow vulnerability. And from the simple truth that when someone realizes their life and their heart already align with your mission, the yes becomes inevitable.

On the contrary, asks can also happen in quieter spaces than a chilly ice rink.

There is a certain kind of restaurant where everything feels softened at the edges. Low lighting. Warm wood. The quiet clink of silverware. A room built for conversation. We sat at a small corner table that required you to lean in if you wanted to hear anything at all. We both ordered something simple. Neither of us pretended the meal was the point.

We had known each other for years, not in a dramatic or accelerated way, but in the steady rhythm of showing up. A call here, a note there, a shared story, a bit of humor when things were heavy. The kind of relationship that grows in layers instead of leaps.

I had not intended to ask that night, and that matters. Some of the most meaningful asks are not planned. They emerge because the room and the breath between words quietly say, now.

We talked about his work, the toll and the pride of it. We talked about aging parents and the ache of roles reversing. We talked about his daughter, the one who carried more weight than people realized.

Then he said something he had never said before. "I want to make sure I leave the world better than I found it. And I want her to see me do it."

He was looking down at his hands, turning his glass slowly on the table. The admission was quiet. But it was a door.

I did not ask for a number. I did not mention naming opportunities. I did not frame a campaign. I simply said, "I know exactly where your gift could live. And I know exactly who it would help."

He looked up. The answer had formed in him long before we sat down. "Yes," he said. "I would like to do that."

Not dramatic. Not grand. Just yes. Yes to legacy. Yes to meaning. Yes to the truth he had finally spoken.

Later, when someone asked me how I made the ask, I said I did not.

Large asks are often what fundraisers fear most, so I want to leave you with one more story.

The naming conversation rarely happens the way people imagine. There was no dramatic pitch deck. No architectural renderings spread like treasure maps. No spotlight on promise.

It was quieter. More measured. More human.

We met in a private conference room with floor to ceiling windows overlooking the city. The sun was setting, turning everything gold before it let go. The donor sat at the head of the table, a quiet posture of authority without dominance. Someone accustomed to carrying responsibility without announcing it.

We talked for a long time about the project and its impact, but what mattered most was not the information. It was the attention. The way we listened to each other.

After a pause, I said, calm and steady, "We're building something that will outlive us all. Something that will reshape care, healing, and belonging. And I believe your name belongs on it."

I did not flinch. I did not shrink. I did not rush to fill the silence. Confidence is not volume. It's stillness.

The donor leaned back. No smile. No reaction. Just thought. Deep and quiet. The kind that slows time. Then they said, "You are asking me to tie my legacy to yours."

I nodded. "Yes. I am."

Not to the organization. Not to the campaign. Not to the building, but to the legacy of what we were shaping together.

Another long silence. Then the donor said, "I need to know that you will still be here when this is real."

The question was not about the project. It was about me.

So I didn't answer with reassurance or promises dressed in confidence. I answered with the truth.

"I'm already here. And I'm not going anywhere."

There was no announcement. No formal close. Just a nod, small and certain. "Let's do it."

The gift that followed changed the scale of what we believed possible. But the yes didn't come from the numbers. It came from belief. Belief in the work.

Belief in the mission. Belief in the person carrying it.

With each of these asks, although the environment was different, the anatomy was the same:

- The Foundation: Relationship/Trust

- The Heartbeat: Story

- The Muscles: Conviction

- The Breath: Silence

- The Hands: Invitation

The takeaway: Every part of an ask must be human-centered.

The anatomy of a big ask isn't about tricks; it's about trust, story, conviction, silence, and invitation. Build those pieces, and the ask won't feel forced.

Chapter Eleven: Journal Prompt

Who will you build your ask for?

- Who is someone you're preparing to ask something of?

- What foundation of trust already exists?

- What story will be the heartbeat of your ask?

- How will you show your conviction?

- Can you practice the power of silence after you ask?

- What invitation will make them feel chosen, not pressured?

Chapter Twelve: When You Fall Flat

Let me tell you a secret: I've bombed.

Not just once. Not just early in my career. Many, many times.

I've walked out of donor meetings where the air was so heavy with awkward silence I wanted to crawl under the table.

I've delivered speeches where the joke fell flat, the story didn't land, or the audience stared at me with polite, blank smiles.

I've made asks that were met with a quick, decisive "No" that cut sharper than I expected.

Every time, I've had to face the same uncomfortable truth: persuasion doesn't always work.

This is the part no one likes to talk about. We tell the stories of the big wins, the record-breaking gifts, the standing ovations. But falling flat happens, and it's okay. When you take big risks, failing is on the table.

I remember one meeting in particular. I had poured myself into the preparation. The case was strong, the donor had capacity, and the timing felt right. I made the ask; and they shut me down instantly. No hesitation. No "Let me think about it." Just "No." I smiled, thanked them, and walked out. But inside, I was gutted.

For days, I replayed every moment. I questioned my delivery, my strategy, even my calling. But slowly I began to understand something. Falling flat was not an ending. It was a signal. It showed me that something was misaligned. Maybe the trust was not strong enough yet. Maybe the story was not the right one.

Maybe the timing was simply not ready.

Persuasion does not rely on perfection. It relies on persistence.

Think about the greatest performers, athletes, or leaders you admire. None of them arrived where they are without failing, sometimes publicly and painfully. What separates them is not that they avoided missteps, but that they stood back up, adjusted, and continued forward with intention.

Falling flat teaches humility, it strips away ego, and it forces you to listen more closely, recalibrate, and find the words or approach that might work next time. Sometimes, falling flat creates space for something even bigger. I've had donors say no to me in one meeting only to circle back months later with a yes twice the size.

Failure also makes you relatable. People aren't persuaded by someone who looks untouchable and perfect. They're persuaded by someone who has been in the trenches, stumbled, and still kept showing up. Vulnerability itself is persuasive.

So when you fall flat, don't let it *define* you. Let it *refine* you.

Because the truth is, persuasion isn't about landing every ask; it's about building the courage to keep asking – even when the last one ended in silence.

There was a major donor meeting early in my career that I believed I had prepared for perfectly. I was confident. I had rehearsed every sentence, memorized the data, the outcomes, and the impact projections. I knew exactly how the conversation should unfold. In my mind, I already had the yes.

The meeting was held in a high-ceilinged private conference room with muted carpet and a long glass table that seemed intentionally designed to amplify silence.

The donor sat across from me, calm, composed, and unreadable. I began speaking, and I could feel myself leaning too far forward, my energy rushing ahead. I was trying to show passion. Instead, I was pushing.

At one point, the donor held up a hand.

"Tim," he said, "you are trying very hard to make *me* believe something. But I'm not sure *you* believe it yet."

The words stopped me cold. I felt heat gather in my chest. Not embarrassment alone. Something deeper. The realization I walked into that room trying to prove something to him, and maybe to myself.

I finished the meeting as gracefully as I could, but when I walked out and sat in my car, I stared at the steering wheel for a long time. The silence felt heavy with everything I wished I had done differently. I was disappointed and embarrassed.

Looking back, I can see the truth. I had been asking from the outside of the work, not from the inside of it. I believed in the mission, but I had not yet let the mission live in me. I was performing conviction rather than embodying it. And there is a difference.

So I stopped rushing to be impressive. I stopped trying to outrun silence. I stopped stacking facts to shield myself from vulnerability. I began to slow down. To speak from the center rather than the edges. To let what I felt lead what I said.

Months later, I met with the same donor again. This time, I didn't bring charts or a speech. I brought myself. I spoke simply and clearly, from the inside.

He listened, nodded once, and said, "There you are." That time, he said, "yes."

The takeaway: Falling flat is feedback.

Failure isn't a dead end; it's a directional sign. Every *no*, every awkward moment, and every flat landing teaches you how to show up stronger, clearer, and more persuasive next time.

Chapter Twelve: Journal Prompt

How do you learn from a failure?

- Recall a time when you fell flat in front of an audience, donor, or colleague. What happened?

- What part of the persuasion "anatomy" (relationship/trust, story, conviction, silence, invitation) might have been missing?

- How did you respond in the moment, and what would you do differently now?

- What did that experience teach you about yourself?

- How might your story of falling flat actually persuade others through your vulnerability?

Chapter Thirteen: Leading with Vulnerability

Imagine someone who asks you to join them in something, and you instinctively want to say yes. What about them persuades you? Is it their confidence? Maybe their authority? Does this person walk into a room and command attention?

While these traits are important in the art of persuasion, the longer I've lived in this work, the more I've discovered that one trait is critical in gaining others' trust and buy-in: vulnerability.

I learned this in the most unexpected of places; not at podiums, but at hospital bedsides, in quiet conversations, in the moments when I didn't have answers. Donors, colleagues, even my team didn't need me to be invincible. They needed me to be real.

Because here's the truth: people aren't persuaded by a mask. They're persuaded by what's behind it.

I once walked into a major donor meeting prepared with every fact and figure. I had rehearsed the pitch a dozen times. But halfway through, the donor stopped me. "Tim," she said, "I already know the numbers. What I want to know is; why does this matter to *you*?"

I froze. My polished speech evaporated.

So I let my guard down. All I could do was tell her the truth: about my mother, about Joni Mitchell, about why being part of a mission that cares for others wasn't just my job, but my life. My voice cracked. My eyes welled. For a moment, I felt exposed; like I had given away too much.

But when I looked up, I saw her leaning in, eyes soft, nodding. That was the moment she decided to give.

Vulnerability is persuasive because it breaks down walls. It says: I trust you with my truth, and I hope you'll trust me with yours. It creates partnership.

As a leader, I've found the same principle holds. Teams don't follow someone who pretends to have it all figured out. They follow someone who admits when they don't. They don't trust perfection; they trust honesty. When I've admitted I was wrong, when I've owned mistakes, when I've said, "I don't know, but I'll figure it out," those have been the moments my leadership was strongest.

Because vulnerability isn't weakness. Vulnerability is courage in its purest form. It's the willingness to risk being seen, to risk rejection, to risk failure.

The most persuasive leaders I know aren't the ones who dominate rooms. They're the ones who open them. Who share their story, their scars, their struggles, and in doing so, make space for others to step forward too.

Leading with vulnerability is the ultimate form of persuasion. Because when people see your heart, they don't just believe in your mission. They believe in you.

The takeaway: Vulnerability is persuasion's secret strength.

People aren't persuaded by perfection; they're persuaded by presence, honesty, and courage. Vulnerability builds trust, deepens connection, and transforms an ask into a shared story.

Chapter Thirteen: Journal Prompt

How do you practice vulnerability?

- Think of a time you let your guard down and it deepened a connection. What happened?

- Where are you currently tempted to hide behind polish instead of showing honesty?

- How might sharing a personal story or struggle make your next ask more persuasive?

- What's one way you could lead with vulnerability this week – with your team, your family, or a donor?

Chapter Fourteen: Relationships Over Transactions

One of the most dangerous myths in fundraising is that success can only be measured by the size of the gift.

Don't get me wrong; gifts matter. They fund the work, build buildings, and ultimately change lives. But if all we ever see is the number on the check, then we've missed the point.

Fundraising is not about transactions; it's about relationships; it's about opening a door that stays open for years.

I've seen fundraisers treat donors like ATM machines. Maybe they get quick wins, but they don't build loyalty.

I've walked alongside donors for years, some who started with modest gifts and grew into transformational donors. Not because I pushed them harder, but because I walked with them longer. Those relationships were built on listening more than asking, remembering birthdays and anniversaries, showing up in hospital waiting rooms, celebrating their children, and grieving their losses.

A donor's relationship with you and your mission could be one of the most meaningful investments of their life.

Relationships also protect you when you fall flat. A donor who trusts you won't walk away after a bad pitch or a mistimed ask. They'll give you another chance because they know you see them as more than a checkbook; you see them as a partner.

And let's be honest: we forget transactions, but we never forget relationships. A donor might not remember the exact amount they gave five years ago, but they'll remember the dinner conversation that made them feel seen. They'll remember the moment you asked about their mother's health or sent a handwritten note after their loss. They'll remember that you cared.

There are donors who become names on a screen and part of your strategy.

Then there are donors who become part of your life; the kind of relationships that soften you, steady you, and shape you.

There is a family I think about often. Our relationship began as they usually do: scheduled meetings, talking points, and presentations.

But during one meeting, we shifted from talking about the hospital and started talking about life. About childhood stories, the parents who shaped us, the love we had lost, the love that had remade us, and the kind of laughter so familiar it feels like a memory, even when it's new.

They became people I trusted. Not because of their generosity, but because of the way they saw me. They saw the parts of me that existed long before I ever became a fundraiser: the boy who once sat in hospital hallways praying for someone he loved to get better, the young man who learned to translate grief into purpose, the human being who believed that caring is not something we do, it's something we are.

At some point, the relationship was no longer anchored by philanthropy. The giving continued, yes, but that was no longer the heart of it.

We celebrated milestones together. We held space in loss. We learned one another's humor, rhythms, impossibilities, and delights.

One day, the wife placed her hand on mine during a conversation about the future of a project that mattered deeply to us both. Her voice softened in that unmistakable way of someone speaking from the center of themselves.

She said, "We're not giving this gift to the hospital. We're giving it with you."

There are moments when your entire vocation crystallizes into one sentence. This was one.

Relationship-based fundraising is human-to-human giving – choosing to build something that lasts together.

They're able to say: "I know these people. I trust this work. I see myself here. I belong in this story."

The greatest responsibility I carry in my work is not the raising of funds. It's stewarding trust, holding relationships with reverence, honoring the humanity of giving, and remembering that every yes comes from a place of personal meaning.

This work has given me many things:

A sense of purpose.

A calling.

A life that feels lived, not observed.

But relationships are the deepest gift of all. Relationships are not the byproduct of the work; they are the work.

They're the reason I will always believe in the power of asking. You are asking for another human to join you, because we are nothing without each other.

The takeaway: Relationships outlast transactions.

A gift is a moment. A relationship is a movement. The real persuasion isn't in the dollars secured, but in the trust built. Transactions are short-term. Relationships are forever.

Chapter Fourteen: Journal Prompt

How are you investing in relationships?

- Who in your professional or personal life have you built a relationship with that goes beyond transaction?

- What did you do to show them they mattered?

- Are there people you've unintentionally treated transactionally? How could you shift that dynamic?

- What small act of presence could deepen a relationship this week?

-

76

Chapter Fifteen: The Donor Bill of Rights

If this work is truly about relationships, then it carries a responsibility, because when giving becomes purely transactional it loses the very thing that makes it meaningful.

I believe we have a responsibility to help people feel connected to our mission, make them feel like they belong, and to help them see how their contribution is integral to our mutual success. This is the least they deserve. To that end, here's my Donor Bill of Rights:

- A donor has the right to be treated as a person first.

- They have the right to understand what they are being invited into and why it matters.

- They have the right to say no without it changing the nature of the relationship.

- They have the right to honesty, even when the truth is less comfortable than a polished version.

- They have the right to feel the impact of what they have supported.

- They have the right to feel something when they give.

The bottom line is that when you treat people with respect, dignity, and honesty, you'll always be more successful in whatever relationships you build.

Joni Mitchell Called Me Ugly

Chapter Sixteen: Case Studies

Here are five case studies to help you begin to recognize and practice the principles in this book. Each one represents a common situation you may find yourself in somewhere along the path of your career.

My hope in presenting these case studies is that you can learn the lesson here, so that when you experience these situations in real life you can recognize them and adjust for the best possible outcome.

Case Study One: When the Story Carried the Ask

I once sat in a meeting where, if you were looking at it objectively, the answer probably should have been no.

There was no long-standing relationship, no deep personal connection to the organization, and no obvious reason for the donor to feel invested. It was the kind of setting where a traditional approach would have felt forced, and everyone in the room seemed to understand that without saying it out loud.

So instead of trying to move the conversation toward a formal pitch, we allowed it to go somewhere more natural.

At one point, a story came up. Not a polished version, not something prepared in advance, but a real moment involving a patient and a family navigating a situation that felt overwhelming and uncertain. There was nothing dramatic about how it was told. It wasn't delivered with emphasis or structure. It was simply shared.

The shift in the room was immediate.

The donor stopped scanning, stopped evaluating, and started listening. You could feel the difference in attention, not because anything had been said more effectively, but because it had been said more honestly.

When the story ended, there was a brief pause. Not uncomfortable, just quiet. Then he asked a single question.

"Does that happen often?"

That question reframed everything.

We were no longer talking about a specific moment. We were talking about how often moments like that exist, how frequently families find themselves in those situations, and what it takes to be prepared for them.

From there, the conversation continued without any need to force it toward an ask. There was no pivot, no structured transition, no formal language that signaled a shift.

A few weeks later, he made a significant gift.

Looking back, it's clear that the decision had already been made in that room, but not because of anything that resembled a traditional ask. It happened because the story created a connection strong enough that the next step felt obvious.

We spend a lot of time thinking about how to ask, but moments like this are a reminder that sometimes the ask is already present. It's embedded in the story, waiting for someone to recognize themselves in it.

The takeaway: People don't give to the institution. They give to what happens because of it.

Case Study Two: The Yes That Didn't Hold

There was a donor who said yes almost immediately. It was one of those meetings where everything seemed to align. The conversation moved quickly, the number was strong, and there was very little resistance. On the surface, it felt like a success.

At the time, everyone left the room feeling energized. It had been efficient, clean, and decisive. But as time passed, it became clear that something had been missing from that moment.

There had been no pause.

No moment where the donor sat with the decision, asked questions, or engaged more deeply with the work. The agreement had been there, but the connection had not.

In the weeks that followed, there was little follow-up engagement. The relationship did not deepen, and the momentum that had felt so promising in the meeting began to fade. Nothing dramatic happened. There was no conflict or clear point of breakdown. The energy simply dissipated.

Looking back, the difference is easy to see.

We had reached agreement, but we had not built alignment.

Agreement can happen quickly. It can feel efficient and productive, but it does not necessarily reflect belief. Alignment takes longer. It requires conversation, curiosity, and a sense that the person understands not just what they are supporting, but why it matters.

Without that foundation, a yes can exist without ever becoming meaningful.

The takeaway: A quick yes can feel good in the moment. A grounded yes is what lasts over time.

Case Study Three: Changing the Conversation in the Room

Not every ask takes place across the table from a donor. Some of the most important moments happen within your own organization.

I remember sitting in a boardroom when a campaign goal was presented. It was a large number, the kind that naturally creates hesitation, even among people who are deeply committed to the work.

At first, no one said anything. But the energy in the room shifted. You could feel people processing it, measuring it against what felt realistic.

Eventually, one board member said what others were thinking. "That doesn't feel realistic."

It was not said with resistance or negativity. It was an honest reaction.

Instead of responding by defending the number or trying to justify it, the conversation moved in a different direction. We stopped focusing on the goal itself and began to talk about what would happen if it was not reached.

What services would not expand. What patients would not receive care. What opportunities would remain out of reach.

As the conversation shifted, the tone of the room changed as well.

It became less about whether the number felt large, and more about whether the work justified the scale of the ask. That shift created clarity, and from that clarity came belief.

Over time, the same individual who had questioned the goal became one of its strongest supporters. Not because they were persuaded through argument, but because they came to see the full picture.

Once that happened, the number was no longer the focus. The outcome was.

The takeaway: Before you ask for a gift, you have to build belief in the work behind it.

Case Study Four: The Long Yes

There was a donor who remained close to the organization for several years without ever making a gift.

He attended events, participated in conversations, and asked thoughtful questions. He was engaged, but he never crossed the line into giving.

At a certain point, it would have been easy to assume that the relationship had reached its limit. In many cases, time and attention would shift elsewhere.

But something about this relationship felt incomplete, so we stayed engaged.

There was no increase in pressure, no attempt to accelerate the timeline. The focus remained on consistency, on continuing to show up, and on allowing the relationship to develop at its own pace.

Over time, that consistency mattered.

Years later, he made a transformational gift. The kind of gift that changes what is possible.

When asked what influenced his decision, his answer was simple: "I wanted to see if you would still be here."

That was the measure.

It was not the strength of the proposal or the urgency of the ask, but the consistency of the relationship over time.

He wanted to know that the commitment existed even when there was no immediate outcome.

The takeaway: Consistency builds trust, and trust is what makes a meaningful yes possible.

Case Study Five: The Ask That Was Too Small

There are moments in this work that stay with you because they reveal something you did not fully see at the time. This was one of those moments.

We were meeting with a donor who had both the capacity and the inclination to make a significant impact. The relationship was strong, the timing felt right, and there was clear alignment with the work. And yet, when it came time to ask, we held back.

The number we presented was lower than what was truly possible. It felt safer, more measured, less likely to create discomfort.

The donor agreed immediately. There was no hesitation. Then, almost as an aside, he said, "I would have done more."

That statement carries weight.

It reflects a missed opportunity, not because the outcome was negative, but because it was incomplete. By asking conservatively, we limited what could have been achieved in that moment.

Sometimes caution feels responsible. It feels like a way to protect the relationship. But in reality, it can prevent the relationship from reaching its full potential.

A well-placed ask is not about pushing too far. It is about recognizing the moment for what it is and responding to it with clarity and confidence.

The takeaway: The right ask reflects both the opportunity and the person's capacity to make an impact.

Case Study Summary: What You Start to See Over Time

Over time, patterns begin to emerge. Not rules or formulas, but tendencies that become clearer with experience.

Some people make decisions quickly, often before the meeting even begins. Others take time, not because they are uncertain, but because they are thoughtful.

Some ask questions as a way to understand the work more deeply. Others ask questions to understand you. And some say very little at all, choosing instead to observe and listen.

These patterns are not something you control. They are something you learn to recognize.

Persuasion is not about directing a conversation toward a specific outcome. It's about understanding the person within that conversation and responding accordingly.

As that understanding grows, the ask itself becomes clearer. Not easier, but more aligned with the moment.

Chapter Seventeen: The Work Beyond the Pages

If you've made it this far, I want to ask you something: *What will this book change for you?*

Not what you learned or what stood out, but can you feel a shift beginning in the way you think about your work, your relationships, and the way you ask.

This book was never meant to just give you information. It was meant to move something: to make you pause, to reconsider how you show up, and to look at the conversations in your life a little differently. That's where this work lives. Not in these pages, but in what you do next. My words may have planted some seeds, but if you want them to grow, they have to be watered. Your practice is the water.

Ways to Practice

If you're using this material with a team, the most valuable thing you can do is move it from discussion into practice. Two ways to practice these concepts are:

1. Facilitate a group discussion
2. Engage in a role-play

Role Playing

To use role playing, you can go back to one of the case studies and assign roles. You can also use a situation you experienced that didn't go as well as you hoped, or one that you're anticipating to be involved in soon. After defining the situation, I'd suggest having at least three roles to act it out: donor, fundraiser, and observer.

After the role play is completed, the observer can facilitate a discussion to encourage constructive feedback and ask how each participant felt about the discussion. Then swap roles and do another role play so each person gets a turn in each role.

Group Discussion

A group discussion is helpful, especially when led by an experienced facilitator. Here are some facilitator notes to begin the discussion. It can start with a simple question to each participant: *"What is one ask you are currently avoiding?"*

Allow each person to answer. Then ask why. Encourage them to go beyond the surface. The first answer is rarely the real one.

From there, have each person say their ask out loud. Not perfectly. Not rehearsed. Just clearly.

Then allow a moment of silence. That space is often where the discomfort lives, but it is also where growth begins.

Invite the group to offer constructive feedback and facilitate discussion as people engage.

Other Ways to Practice

Practice saying your ask out loud before you walk into the room. Become comfortable hearing yourself say it. When you make the ask, allow space for a response. Do not rush to fill the silence.

Ensure that your story stands on its own, even without supporting data. And take the time to understand the people you're engaging with, not just in terms of their giving, but in terms of who they are.

Learn to Recognize the Moments That Stay With You

There are moments in this work that remain long after the details have faded:

- A comment that reframes everything.

- A moment of connection that was not planned.

- A conversation where the outcome became clear before it was spoken.

- I once heard a donor say, "I don't give because I have to. I give because I get to." That distinction is important.

- Another said, "You make me feel like I belong." That is the goal.

These are the moments that define the work. Not the numbers, but the meaning behind them. When you can recognize them, you can begin to facilitate them.

Final Thoughts on Practice

There is no perfect approach to this work, no script that guarantees a specific outcome, and no way to remove uncertainty from the process. What matters is the willingness to engage, to listen, and to ask.

Practicing with your coworkers — or even on your own — will build confidence and help prevent unforced errors. Not because the outcomes become predictable, but because the process becomes familiar.

Eventually, the hesitation begins to fade. Not entirely, but enough that it no longer prevents action. Because the most important step is not getting the answer, it's asking the question.

Chapter Eighteen: The Final Circle

As I close this book – a book stitched together from Broadway stages, donor stories, bold asks, Joni Mitchell letters, leadership lessons, miracles, risks, heartbreaks, and wild leaps of faith – I find myself thinking about you, the reader who made it to the end.

Together, we've explored:

- Joni Mitchell and the courage to ask the impossible.

- Broadway and the power of timing, storytelling, and connection.

- Donors who changed lives with a single moment of generosity.

- My mother, who taught me heart-first leadership.

- Ernestine, who taught me fire, truth, and fearless love.

- Sarah, who taught me grace, acceptance, and warmth.

- The calls I made that took everything I had.

- The meetings that changed the direction of my life.

- The asks that felt too bold until they became yeses.

- The quiet moments that shaped the loud ones.

You now carry these lessons with you; not because I'm right, or because my way is the only way, but because you deserve to live and lead and love with passion, with heart, with courage, with authenticity, and with a fire of your own.

My hope, as you close these pages, is simple: do not let this story stay here. Take it with you. Apply it to your work, your relationships, your leadership, your dreams, your community, and let it inspire your wildest, boldest, most unimaginable asks.

Be brave.

Be warm.

Be curious.

Be human.

Be willing to step into rooms where you don't feel ready and speak anyway. Carry forward the lessons:

Ask boldly.

Love deeply.

Lead with your heart first.

Trust that the right people will appear. Know that vulnerability is strength.

And remember that the most powerful persuasion tool you have is your humanity.

If you lead with heart, ask with courage, and love without hesitation, the people you need will always find you, exactly when you're ready for them.

And so here we are, at the end, which is not an ending at all. For you, it's actually the beginning. Because life, like Joni once sang, is a carousel – round and round we travel: revisiting old lessons, discovering new ones, and returning to ourselves again and again, older, wiser, braver, and kinder.

The circle keeps turning, and so do we.

So, let me ask you to consider this:

All these pages and all these stories have brought you to one simple truth: the world is moved forward by the brave ones who dare to speak first.

I want you to think of the one thing that keeps tugging at your heart: the one dream, the one conversation, the one truth you've tucked away because it feels too big, too risky, or too exposed.

That's your ask. Not tomorrow. Not when you feel ready. Not when the stars align. Now.

Even if your voice shakes. Even if your hands tremble. *Especially then.* Because the life you want isn't hiding from you; it's waiting for you.

And you already know how.

The ~~End~~ Beginning.

About the Author

TIMOTHY BOYNTON is an award-wining health-care philanthropist, senior executive, and creative force who has helped raise more than $200 million for mission-driven organizations. he currently serves as Senior Vice President and Chief Development Officer and Chief PR and communications officer at Lakeland Regional Health, where he has led transformational fundraising campaigns.

Before stepping into the world of healthcare philanthropy, Boynton built his career on Broadway where he worked behind the scenes as a personal assistant to writers and producers. That unlikely bridge between the arts and philanthropy shaped his distinctive ability to connect, persuade, and inspire. Since then, his work has earned international recognition, including honors from Modern Healthcare and the Association for Healthcare Philanthropy as one of the world's leading fundraisers.

His path has been supported and inspired by some of today's most influential voices in film, music, and theater, including Jay Leno, Brooke Shields, Trisha Yearwood, Molly Shannon, and Julianna Margulies, several of whom have offered words of encouragement and endorsement along his journey.

Boynton is known not only for the scale of his success, but for the heart behind it. His approach to fundraising is rooted in genuine relationships, trust, communication, and the bold belief in the power of the ask. He believes that generosity is not simply about money, but about courage, vulnerability, timing, and connection.

Through his book, ***Joni Mitchell Called Me Ugly***, he invites readers into the real stories, humorous missteps, and transformative moments that shaped him, offering both inspiration and practical tools for anyone ready to step into their voice, ask for what they want, and create impact in their world. He lives in Florida with his husband, Alvin, and their beloved dog, Piglet, and continues to blend his passion for the arts, storytelling, and community advancement in everything he creates.

You can learn more about Timothy Boynton at timothyboynton.com.